Reignite

A practical guide to reigniting your spark and
restoring your complete wellbeing

How to get from busy and exhausted to energised and balanced

Victoria Jones

The journey of a thousand
miles begins with one step.

Loa Tzu

Contents

Welcome

Hormones influence EVERYTHING that happens in your body: your mood, sleep, weight and energy are all controlled by your hormones.

ALL hormones work together, if one is out of balance there will be a cascade of unbalance though the entire endocrine system, which in turn can cause hormonal symptoms and wellbeing niggles.

Whilst it **is** most likely your hormones that are causing the symptoms and niggles that you may be experiencing, or normalising, it is actually them simply telling you that they are out of balance.

Hormonal symptoms are common but they are NOT normal.

Yet, and particularly during our late 30's and early 40's, these wellbeing niggles and increasing hormonal symptoms are normalised because 'it's just my age' or 'it's just my hormones'.

Please believe me when I say, it's not.

Any problematic hormonal symptoms you are experiencing are showing up for a reason. They are your body's way of telling you that it is out of balance and lacking in something that it needs.

This can often be something simple, maybe deeper nourishment, movement or rest and relaxation, all of which can calm and change the environment that your hormones are in.

In our late 40's we accept that the menopause is on the horizon and because of the negative exposure it has had over the years, we believe it's going to get a whole lot worse and there is little we can do about it.

I do have an education in the peri to post menopause life phase, however this guide is very much about the years before.

Those years when we don't tend to give our hormones any serious thought, despite often noticing that symptoms during our cycle are different or changing.

Those years when we are too busy to really acknowledge the changes.

Those years when you might not even be paying any attention to your cycle but you just know that you're exhausted, frustrated and the diets and intense workouts you are doing are having absolutely no effect... oh, and you might be having the mildest hot flush during the night!

Sound familiar?

Now that's not to say that if you are menopausal right now or even post-menopausal this guide won't be of value to you. Symptoms don't always stop post menopause and, if they do, other (often totally avoidable) health issues and wellbeing niggles can show up which are just as troublesome.

Prevention is always better than cure and I am a firm believer that the more we know the better we do. The earlier we know, the sooner we do it BUT it's never too late to make a change, to make an improvement or to create lifestyle habits to support or improve our wellbeing.

There is no 'one size fits all' solution to hormonal imbalance, although you do need to consider a whole-body approach. You also do not need to wait until symptoms show up to start to support your hormones or wellbeing.

I know how busy women are. Juggling careers, running homes, honouring family and social commitments, raising children, caring for aging parents – ultimately trying to be all things to all people. Becoming human doings rather than human beings, spinning all the plates and as a result, becoming more exhausted, disconnected and stuck in a state of survival.

When we get too busy for ourselves and our health, happiness and wellbeing, the thought of change feels like an overwhelming mission that is often coated in guilt. This is why I have created this wellbeing guide. The information, activities and strategies that I share here are simple, stackable and sustainable. But don't be fooled, the few minutes they might take to implement, reflect on or consider will have a hugely positive impact.

There will, most likely, be so many things in this guide that you already know to do, but you must do what you know. Rather than simply reading through the pages, being reminded of things you know or that you used to do once, but not actually implementing or re-introducing them when you close the guide, I have added in a lot of… interactive pages.

There are checklists, spaces to plan and pages for you to simply complete. I have always thought that if nothing changes then nothing changes but more recently I have realised that if nothing changes, nothing will improve. If we don't take the action we need, in any area, then things will get progressively worse.

The brain also loves it when we achieve something or it can see us making progress. Every time you accomplish something on an interactive page and tick it off, your brain will release the feel-good hormone, dopamine.

The more you activate the release of dopamine, the more your brain will want you to repeat the associated action or behaviour. Before you know it, you'll have new habits in place that are automatic and you'll feel better for them, mentally as well as physically.

Now is the time to value your health and wellbeing above all else. To put the work in and implement simple lifestyle strategies and create small but effective habits that will make a real difference to how you feel.

I truly believe in a whole-body approach, nourishing your body in the right way for you to balance your hormones because then EVERYTHING changes.

√ You wake up feeling energised after a great night's sleep and don't need to fuel up on coffee just to face the day.

√ You have tons of energy and afternoon naps become a thing of the past.

√ That stubborn weight gain that you tried to shift for years finally melts away.

√ You feel like yourself again and have so much confidence.

√ You're calmer and more resilient to life.

I'm so excited for you to discover how amazing you can feel when your hormones are working for you, rather than against you, and how simple it can be to start to rewrite your own health and wellbeing story.

Phase one

<u>Identify and manage your stress</u>

The biggest consideration for our wellbeing and hormonal health is stress.

Before I delve in to this one, though, I want to share some simple but important neuroscience and biology facts.

The stress response begins in the part of the brain called the amygdala.

When it anticipates or perceives a danger, the amygdala sends a distress signal to the hypothalamus (in a different part of the brain) which tells the adrenal glands (that sit just on top of the kidneys) to release the stress hormone cortisol.

This communication triggers a very fast cascade of hormonal reactions and physiological changes that we know as the 'fight or flight' response, activated by the sympathetic nervous system.

The heart beats faster, the pulse and blood pressure rise, breathing becomes quicker, alertness in the brain and senses increase and glucose and fat (from your stores) supply energy to every part of your body for you to fight the danger or run from it to safety.

Prehistorically that danger would have been a sabre tooth tiger. The brain would activate the fight or flight response for you to fight the tiger or flee to the safety of your cave. Once safe, the **para**sympathetic nervous system would activate the 'rest and digest' response, calming the physiological changes and resetting the hormonal reactions.

Of course, life has evolved, and the sabre tooth tiger is no longer our greatest life-threatening danger. There are so many other things we react to or anticipate as a danger and, whilst most of them are not life-threatening dangers, the body respond to them as though they are.

Not all stress is obvious and there are three main types:

Physical stress

> Injury, illness, inflammation in the body, food choices and over exercising can all activate our stress response, as can hormonal changes.

Emotional stress

> Childhood trauma, busy home or work life, current fears and worries around finances, health, older parents, young children or work can all trigger the stress response, as can the upset around relationship breakdowns, loss or loneliness.

Environmental stress

> This is probably the most hidden stressor in our lifestyle but we live in a highly toxic world. We are surrounded by chemicals in our skincare and beauty products, our cleaning products, our food and plastics. Artificial light and air pollution also cause a stress response.

So many women are constantly dealing with a combination of these stressors, day in and day out. Whilst in isolation they are all relatively low-level factors, the continuous build up can, over time, put our body into a state of chronic stress.

This chronic stress not only causes a range of troublesome symptoms but because our bodies will always prioritise survival over reproduction, if the stress hormone cortisol is continually released, the production of the main sex hormones is, in turn, compromised.

This triggers further disruption through our entire endocrine system, ultimately creating even more imbalance to our health and wellbeing.

Some symptoms of stress are similar to those associated with declining sex hormones, including brain fog, memory loss, low libido, anxiety, insomnia and digestive problems or food sensitivities.

Untreated low-level chronic stress can also lead to problems with infertility, heart disease, metabolic and thyroid function, problems regulating the heart rate and much more serious disease (dis-ease in the body).

Whilst I strongly recommend you reduce your exposure to environmental stressors, you also need to learn how to MANAGE your own physical and emotional stress.

Again there is no 'one size fits all' for this and I hate to be the bearer of more bad news but a large glass of wine and bar of chocolate whilst scrolling through social media is NOT a stress management strategy. It is just another way to produce even more cortisol.

Manging stress means ACTIVELY de-stressing EVERYDAY to bring the sympathetic and parasympathetic nervous systems into balance. This brings the body out of the 'fight or flight' state and into the 'rest and digest' state.

As I've outlined, the adrenal glands are responsible for releasing the stress hormone, cortisol, when the brain anticipates a danger but they do so much more.

The adrenals are the foundation of hormonal balance, producing the DHEA hormone which is the pre-curser for the main sex hormones, estrogen, testosterone and progesterone. They help to regulate your blood sugar level and burn fat but they are also the back-up for producing the sex hormones when the ovaries begin to slow down as we age.

If the adrenals are exhausted from constantly producing cortisol during your 30's and into your 40's, they have nothing to give when needed later on. This means it is vital that you prioritise your adrenal health as early as possible.

When the adrenals are out of balance you may find yourself:

- Getting a second wind at 10pm
- Waking up at 2am
- Reaching for a large glass of wine each evening in an attempt to quieten or distract your busy mind
- Grabbing sweet sugary snacks mid-afternoon to give you enough energy to get through the rest of the day

You may also experience:

- Chronic headaches
- Wounds that don't heal
- Difficulty waking up in the morning
- Fatigue or low energy
- Acne or other skin problems
- Low mood or irritability

Restoring and supporting your adrenal health is vital for your wellbeing but it does take time. If your adrenals have been working flat out for the past 20 years, responding to continual low-level stresses, they will not repair overnight.

It will take months, maybe even a year or more, but please believe me when I say it is worth giving them your attention and the support they need, particularly if you are in your late 30s or early 40s. If you start to do the work now you will have the strongest foundations when you really need it.

Learning to identify, reduce or eliminate and actively manage your stress is, in my opinion, the most important thing you can do for your wellbeing. Yet it can be the hardest, though it really doesn't need to be.

"Win the morning, you win the day"

Tim Ferriss

How you begin your day can impact your mood, mindset, your hormones and adrenal health.

The first 20 – 30 minutes after waking are so important. Our cortisol levels spike shortly after waking up so if you snooze your alarm (because you are exhausted from a night of poor sleep) and then get out of bed late, rushing about getting ready, grabbing a couple of cups of coffee to wake you up as you check your social media or emails with one hand, making the lunch with other whilst listening to the news and shovelling a bowl of something down your throat before you fly out of the door, your cortisol levels will go through the roof. Each of these things produce more and more cortisol, raising your levels up and up and up.

A morning routine doesn't need to be long and complicated. It does, however, need to allow the naturally raised cortisol levels the chance to settle, before you get caught up into your day and face more of your hidden stressors (situations, activities and emotions). That's those situations that cause the stress response in you.

Your cortisol may still build up through the day BUT it will build from a low base line rather than on top of an already elevated level.

Here are my favourite activities for a morning routine, but please know that you don't have to do them all or spend an hour on each one. Simply spending 10 minutes on a couple of these activities (or similar) will be a game changer. Of course, you don't have to do everything I am about suggest tomorrow. If you are currently waking up exhausted then you first need to address your sleep (see phase three) then try to just get up 10 minutes earlier tomorrow and for the next week and do one of the morning routine activities.

Remember how I said earlier that the brain loves it when we achieve something? It is so much better to look back and say 'I got up 10 minutes earlier EVERY day this week and did [insert your morning routine activity of choice here] instead of 'I got up an hour earlier once this week and then failed the rest of the days".

One final thing before I share my favourite morning routine activities. We are basically houseplants with emotions, we need sunlight and we need water.

You might not feel it, but when you wake up after your restorative seven - nine hours sleep, you are naturally de-hydrated so a glass of water first thing (yes before your first cuppa!) is so important. It not only re-hydrates you but will increase alertness and kick start your metabolism which, unsurprisingly, can be slowed by chronic stress.

Morning routine activities

Visualisation, meditation, breathwork and affirmations

Any of these activities will focus your attention and, in turn, reduce busy thoughts and chatter in the brain that may be triggering an emotional stress response. You do not have to do all of these and just a few minutes of any will have a positive impact.

There are apps such as Calm and Headspace that you can download and listen to, but please don't be tempted to 'quickly check your emails or social media' when you go to launch the app. That will not have the same positive impact.

If you are comfortable to, you can simply set a timer for three or five minutes and sit in silence focusing just on your breath. If your mind wanders or gets stuck focusing on a thought, bring your attentions back to your breath. You may need to do that a dozen or more times during your first meditation but with practice, your mind will learn to just let the thoughts pass without giving them any attention.

Exercise

All movement is wonderful and our body is designed to move every day. Exercise doesn't need to be a high impact aerobics class, 60-minute gym session or a 5k run. A daily 10-minute weights workout, yoga flow or walk around the block are often much more effective, particularly if your adrenals are weary.

Reading

As with the visualisations, meditation, breathwork and affirmations activity, reading will focus your attention to quieten the busyness in the brain. It doesn't matter what you chose to read; personal development, an autobiography or fiction but please pick up a book every day. That's a real book with real pages if you can.

Journaling or colouring

As with some of the other activities, each of these encourage you to focus your attention and, if you opt for the journaling, also your thoughts. Journaling helps to organise your thoughts, worries and dreams. There is no right or wrong way to journal. Simply writing all your thoughts onto paper in a list brings you clarity and lightens the load you are carrying in your mind. Once on paper it is often easier to realise your next best step or that things are not as big a worry as you thought when they were just in your head. If journaling isn't for you then grab some crayons or pens and spend 10 minutes colouring in or just doodling.

Morning routine checklist

●	Drink a glass of water	
🫁	Visualisations, meditation, breathwork or affirmations	2 – 5 mins
🏋	Exercise	8 – 12 mins
📚	Reading	5 - 10 mins
✏	Journaling or colouring	5 - 10 mins

Date / day started:

Morning routine checklist

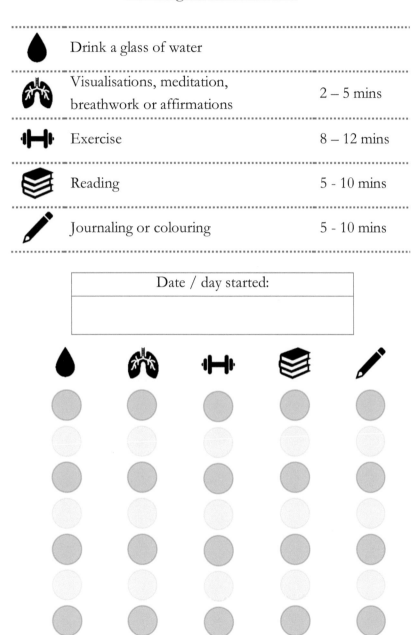

💧	Drink a glass of water	
🫁	Visualisations, meditation, breathwork or affirmations	2 – 5 mins
🏋️	Exercise	8 – 12 mins
📚	Reading	5 - 10 mins
✏️	Journaling or colouring	5 - 10 mins

Date / day started:

Morning routine checklist

⬤	Drink a glass of water	
🫁	Visualisations, meditation, breathwork or affirmations	2 – 5 mins
🏋	Exercise	8 – 12 mins
📚	Reading	5 - 10 mins
✏	Journaling or colouring	5 - 10 mins

Date / day started:

⬤	🫁	🏋	📚	✏
◯	◯	◯	◯	◯
◯	◯	◯	◯	◯
◯	◯	◯	◯	◯
◯	◯	◯	◯	◯
◯	◯	◯	◯	◯
◯	◯	◯	◯	◯
◯	◯	◯	◯	◯

Morning routine checklist

●	Drink a glass of water	
(lungs)	Visualisations, meditation, breathwork or affirmations	2 – 5 mins
(dumbbell)	Exercise	8 – 12 mins
(books)	Reading	5 - 10 mins
(pencil)	Journaling or colouring	5 - 10 mins

Date / day started:

Morning routine checklist

💧	Drink a glass of water	
🫁	Visualisations, meditation, breathwork or affirmations	2 – 5 mins
🏋	Exercise	8 – 12 mins
📚	Reading	5 - 10 mins
✏	Journaling or colouring	5 - 10 mins

Date / day started:

Morning routine checklist

💧	Drink a glass of water	
🫁	Visualisations, meditation, breathwork or affirmations	2 – 5 mins
🏋	Exercise	8 – 12 mins
📚	Reading	5 - 10 mins
✏	Journaling or colouring	5 - 10 mins

Date / day started:

💧	🫁	🏋	📚	✏
⚪	⚪	⚪	⚪	⚪
⚪	⚪	⚪	⚪	⚪
⚪	⚪	⚪	⚪	⚪
⚪	⚪	⚪	⚪	⚪
⚪	⚪	⚪	⚪	⚪
⚪	⚪	⚪	⚪	⚪
⚪	⚪	⚪	⚪	⚪

"It's not the stress that breaks us but the way we carry it"

Unknown

Whilst I would love to tell you that a morning routine alone will restore the balance of your elevated stress hormone and repair the disruption that it causes, I must instead remind you that manging stress means ACTIVELY de-stressing EVERYDAY; bringing the sympathetic and parasympathetic nervous systems into balance.

There is a plethora of strategies for actively de-stressing but because there is no 'one size fits all', you will need to experiment to find the one(s) that work for you.

That said, below are some of my favourites which you might like to explore and expand on. As with the morning routine, you don't need to do ALL the strategies that I suggest over the following pages. Please take inspiration and regularly use the ones that work for you throughout your day.

Breathe fully and deeply

Breathing is the fastest way to restore balance between the two sides of the nervous system which, as I'm sure you've realised by now, is the key to calming and quietening the whole body and bringing it into a restful and relaxed state.

When we are exposed to stress, we breathe faster, naturally taking short and shallow breaths from the chest. Our shoulders also tend to move closer to our ears as we tense up. How often have you experienced a tension headache, a stiff neck or tight shoulders during a stressful day or period of your life?

How often have you blamed that tension headache, a stiff neck or tight shoulders on a poor night of sleep, because you were lying there wide awake at 2am and it must be your pillow?

There are so many breathing techniques that you can use including the 4 4 4 or 4 7 8 technique, pursed-lip breathing and alternate-nostril breathing (nadi sodhana).

There is an abundance of guided breathing practices you can follow online or through apps but I'm going to share my two favourite techniques with you here.

Belly breathing

- Place one hand on your chest and the other hand on your belly.
- Allow your belly to relax (no squeezing or clenching your muscles).
- Breathe in slowly through your nose – you should you feel your belly rise.
- Breath out slowly through your nose – you should feel your belly fall.
- The hand on your chest should remain relatively still.

Square breathing (this is my personal favourite)

You are going to visualise a square or if you have a pen and paper to hand you can draw the square.

- Starting in the top left corner take a breath in and visualise travelling along / draw the top of a square.
- Breath out visualise / draw the right side of the square.
- Breathe in and visualise / draw the bottom of the square.
- Breathe out and visualise / draw the left side of the square taking you back to the start point.

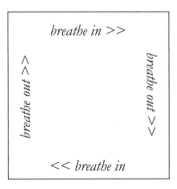

Work to lengthen the breath so the square gets bigger but with all four sides the same length to create a perfect shape.

Whichever breathing exercise you favour, I encourage you to practice it throughout your day and not just in times of obvious stress or anxiety. Pick a daily task that you repeat regularly - it can be boiling the kettle, getting a glass of water or spending a penny - and while you are at that task, check in with your breathing, place your hand on your stomach or visualise your square and just complete a few conscious breath cycles. Spend a few extra minutes (two to five minutes) first thing in the morning and last thing at night and you will notice such a positive effect and feel so much calmer.

Go outside

When you are in busy environments the brain is always looking for danger, so step outside WITHOUT your device, ideally into green open space and breathe. Focus on the sounds you can hear or the colours you see.

Switch off electronic devices

Switch off the electronic devices, media and negative noise. Much of what we see and hear can cause the perceived stress I mentioned so have a regular digital detox. When you are scrolling through social media, make sure you are following positive accounts that uplift and inspire you. Limit how often you watch, listen to, or read the news. Instead, use the time you might normally spend doing that on different activities that nourish your wellbeing.

Be creative

Studies have shown that most people who try art as a form of stress relief experience significant reductions in their cortisol levels.

You don't have to be an artist or know how to draw or paint to reap the benefits of art and there are so many forms that you can experiment with including: ceramics and clay work, scrapbooking, collage or decoupage, knitting, sewing, crochet, cross stitch, painting, drawing or doodling and even simply colouring in.

When we are chronically stressed the thought of finding time to get creative can seem impossible but just 10 minutes can have a huge impact, particularly if you follow the advice that was gifted to me by the wonderful Donna Maxine at White Thyme in Dorset.

Donna shared that colouring in with your **non-dominant** hand for just 5-10 minutes is as effective as completing a 20-minute deep meditation!

There are many other benefits for our cognitive health that are stimulated by using your non-dominant hand but right now I am sharing this strategy to encourage you to **actively de-stress**, by bringing both sides of the nervous system back into balance.

There is an abundance of adult colouring books and magazines available and even free images online that you can download and print. However, to save you time searching I am honoured to share this image drawn by the beautiful Christa Mav for you to colour now.

Christa is a London based artist who has a passion for creating and sharing with others her own unique style and creativity. You can find more about Christa and her artwork on her website: www.christamav.com.

Practice meditation

Meditation is increasing in popularity as more people notice the many health benefits it provides and explore ways to reduce and manage stress in our fast-paced modern world.

There is a vast range of meditation styles available to you, including silent, visualisation, movement, mantra and mindfulness. You can use apps or streaming platforms to follow a meditation, simply sit in silence having set a timer colour in with the non-dominant hand, as I just mentioned. This is as much a form of mindful meditation, as is walking in nature.

Not all styles of meditation are right for everyone and, as with everything I have already shared, you need to find the style that works for YOU. An element of perseverance may be required when you first start out. It is usual for anyone new to meditation to notice their mind wandering and that they focus on a passing thought. If this happens, bring your focus back to your breath or the words of the mantra or the image you are visualising. You may have to bring your focus back a dozen times initially but the more you repeat a meditation the stiller your mind will become for longer and your thoughts will become like clouds, simply floating by without taking your attention.

Schedule your 'Tiara Time'

I first heard about 'Tiara Time' from Jenny Burrell, the head of Burrell Education and I have spoken about it and encouraged my own clients to put their tiaras on ever since.

'Tiara Time' is simply YOU time. It is scheduling in the hobbies that you always want to do, but never have time for. It is making time for the activities that fill your mind, body and soul with happiness. It is the simple things that take you away from the juggling and trying to be all things to all people.

'Tiara Time' isn't the big adventures, it is the simple things that you can dip into for 20 minute a day or an hour or two a week and that make you happy and switch off. Maybe the creative things I spoke about a few pages ago, reading, gardening, taking a class or learning a new skill. What 'Tiara Time' looks like is totally up to you, but it needs to be scheduled in as a non-negotiable daily or weekly task.

Connect with others

We are social beings and are wired to connect and spend time with others. Connecting with the right people can help us feel happier, more secure and can give us a greater sense of purpose – all of which help us to manage stress.

Do be aware, though, of connections that add stress rather than reduce it. The meet-ups through obligation or that drain your energy need to be few and far between. Spend more time connecting with a few good friends who support and encourage you, who you can trust, laugh and be yourself with - and vice versa.

Social bonding and physical contact, including hugging, kissing, holding hands and sexual intimacy can all activate the production of the hormone oxytocin. Although oxytocin plays an important role in reproduction it is also a natural stress reliever, stimulating relaxation and lowering anxiety when levels rise.

Balance your blood sugar throughout the day

I will talk about this a little more later in this guide but want to emphasise here the importance of balancing your blood sugar level throughout the day. This will prevent extra cortisol being released to stabilise any blood sugar dips or spikes that occur. These dips often tell you to reach for the chocolate or caffeine as a 'pick me up' mid-afternoon and the blood sugar spikes happen when you listen to the dips and act on them.

Wellness wisdom from phase one

Start a morning routine tomorrow. Set your alarm 10 minutes earlier than usual and complete at least one or two of the activities on the morning routine checklist.

Make it a mission to actively de-stress every day. Schedule 'Tiara Time' into your diary as non-negotiable.

Pick a task that you already repeat regularly throughout the day and check it with your breathing pattern each time you complete that chosen task.

Phase two:

<u>Calm and nourish your gut</u>

Gut health is a mammoth subject and I am only going to skim the surface and share the most important information in this phase. Don't be deceived though, implementing the recommendations I'm about to make, although simple, will have a hugely positive impact on your gut, hormones and overall health.

In our gut there are trillions of bacteria that make up the gut microbiome, which:

- Aid digestion
- Remove toxins
- Keep the immune system strong
- Influence weight and mood

Many of our lifestyle choices impact our gut bacteria, unfortunately, all too often destroying the good and making space for the bad bacteria to thrive, which causes inflammation. This inflammation initially causes its own cascade of symptoms which are often brushed off, normalised or labelled as hormonal, including skin problems and fragmented sleep.

Of course, there may be times when your fragmented sleep is a more direct result of your hormones, but even then many imbalances are not specifically because of hormones but because of the environment your hormones are in. I'm sure you've already realised from the previous phase that stress can cause and worsen hormonal symptoms and wellbeing niggles. Poor gut health triggers the same outcomes in addition to a stress response.

The food we eat, or more importantly absorb, sustains our hormones and their environment and so what we eat it is a vital start point for our complete wellbeing.

You really do need to become your own diet detective. Pay attention to how you feel after eating different food sources and after each meal. If you don't feel energised, satisfied and comfortable after you eat, perhaps you may need to adjust your choices?

Even if you've been eating a particular food source all your life without any reaction, if you do start to notice a reaction, consider reducing or eliminating it. Our bodies continually change and we can develop an intolerance without rhyme or reason, or in times of chronic stress.

There really is no great secret or complicated strategy when it comes to basic gut health, the key is to simply… **Cook and eat REAL food**.... most of the time!

Support your gut and feed the good bacteria by eating a less acidic diet, eat more plant-based food and get your food from as close to source as possible.

Eat more vegetables than fruit, especially cooked cruciferous veggies including; broccoli, cauliflower, cabbage, brussel sprouts and kale.

Add whole foods with lots of vitamins and minerals. Increase magnesium to repair any damage to the gut lining and get sufficient vitamins C, D and K in daily. I am personally not a huge fan of taking off the shelf multi-supplements 'just because' and always encourage sourcing vitamins and minerals in a natural form where possible.

Magnesium can be found in whole grains, nuts, seeds, chickpeas, lentils, dark green leafy vegetables and chocolate, though it must be a dark not milk variety.

Citrus and kiwi fruit, red peppers and broccoli contain high sources of vitamin C.

Vitamin K, found in dark green leafy vegetables, is vital for the absorption of vitamin D (and calcium). The highest food sources of vitamin D include eggs, ricotta cheese, tofu, oily fish and mushrooms though the best source of vitamin D is sunshine. Most of us should be able to get sufficient exposure to the sun without risking skin damage.

You may find it beneficial to supplement these four vitamins (although D is a hormone which I'll explain more in phase four) and, of course, there are always individual circumstances and situations when additional vitamin supplementation may be required. I urge you though, when this is the case, to fully research and source a good quality natural product. Many of the 'off the shelf' brands contain more emulsifier than vitamin. If you take a vitamin D supplement, for example, then ensure it either contains vitamin K2 or you are eating plenty of dark green leafy veg.

"Fat loss is about hormones NOT calories"

unknown

It breaks my heart when I hear women talking about counting calories, skipping meals or following another restrictive diet in an attempt to lose weight or drop a dress size.

I shared previously that the adrenals help to regulate your blood sugar level and burn fat. If fat loss is your goal you really do need to start on the inside by calming and repairing your adrenals and eating to balance your blood sugar.

Spikes and dips in your blood sugar will trigger a stress response which, as you now know, will burden the adrenals. These erratic blood sugar changes are caused by skipping or leaving too long between meals or reaching for the sugar rich and high carbohydrate snacks – the ones we crave for a quick energy boost when our blood sugar level drops too low. Eating protein at every meal will help keep you fuller for longer and your blood sugar level better stabilised.

I'll mention this again in the nurturing happy hormones phase but the main sex hormones and vitamin D are fat derived and need good fats for their production. Therefore, not only do you need calm your gut, you should also stay away from anything artificial, diet or low fat. As much as possible, avoid processed foods and excessive refined sugars.

Instead, increase your intake of good fats, quality protein and fibre; aim to eat these sources at every meal.

Good Fat
- Oily fish; salmon, trout, mackerel, sardines, herring
- Eggs
- Nuts; almond, cashew, hazelnut
- Seeds; sunflower, sesame, pumpkin, flax, chia
- Avocado
- Grass fed butter

- Natural peanut butter - keep portions in check with this one (1tbsp for a snack).
- Olive oil – for dressings
- Coconut oil – for cooking

Quality Protein
- Oily fish; salmon, trout, mackerel, sardines, herring
- White fish; cod, haddock
- Grass fed meat / Free range chicken
- Cheese; hard cheeses, goats, feta
- Eggs
- Beans
- Nuts and seeds
- Quinoa
- Organic Soy (if you can tolerate it)
- Lentils and pulses.
- Dark green leafy vegetables

Fibre
- Wholegrains
- Fruit and vegetables
- Chickpeas
- Nuts and seeds
- Beans and lentils

Dairy, wheat and sugar can cause sensitivity to the digestive system which, as a result, can clog rather than cleanse. In turn this unbalances hormones and unsettles your gut microbiome. You may wish to reduce or eliminate these food sources for up to a month then re-introduce them. Add each source back in, one per week and then notice how your body feels for the following three days.

Aim to snack on nuts and seeds or add in extra nutrients by drinking a green juice, which is particularly helpful if you suffer from a mid-afternoon energy slump.

Avoid the trans fats which are found in processed foods, margarine, sunflower and vegetable oil. Steer clear from oils high in omega-6 fats and load up on rich sources of natural omega-3s instead (oily fish, flaxseed, chia seeds, walnuts and grass-fed animal products).

There is no such thing as good or bad, treat or cheat food. There is simply food. Some food will nourish you and support hormonal balance, your gut microbiome and, in return, your complete wellbeing. Some food will make you feel sluggish, tired or uncomfortable, sometimes immediately after eating and sometimes a day or two later. You really do need to find out which foods affect you in which way.

Rather than restricting, I always encourage my clients to add in more of the nourishing foods to crowd out the foods that slow you down. Your gut microbiome will change quickly and you will naturally start to crave more of the alkaline foods which feed the good bacteria and reduce inflammation.

"Your gut is NOT Las Vegas…

What happens in the gut does not stay in the gut!"

unknown

As well as calming and nourishing the gut by reducing stress and inflammation and crowding out the sources that feed the bad bacteria, it is vital you support your liver.

Amongst many other things, the liver breaks down the food you eat and converts it into energy, helping the body to get rid of toxins and waste. It also plays an essential role in regulating the balance of the sex and thyroid hormones, removing any excess from the body. If the liver can't do this properly there is the risk of a hormone dominance which will cause an imbalance throughout the rest of the hormones. Remember, all hormones work together.

Pay attention to your bowel movement because this can tell you so much about your liver function and overall health. The bowel is an organ of habit, it loves to empty in the same toilet of the same house and at around the same time each and (hopefully) every day. The bowel does not like change. Have you ever noticed that when you are away from home it takes a few days for your bowels to relax? Ideally you will be having a bowel movement every day but less than three bowel movements a week or more than three a day are regarded as abnormal. Your stool should be smooth and soft, like a sausage or snake.

When it comes to your liver and bowel movement, please don't neglect the basics.

Drink water

> Aim to drink two – three litres of water every day. Tea (unless herbal) and coffee do not count towards your water total and PLEASE don't avoid drinking enough water through fear of leakage. Pelvic floor issues are common but not normal, they can be rectified so find yourself a pelvic health physio, address your issues and stay hydrated.

Eat well

The suggestions on the previous pages are the key to this but ensure you include fibre at each meal, ideally from fruit and vegetables (more vegetable than fruit).

Loading up on dark green leafy veg will keep things moving along in the digestive system and help with cleaning out any build-up of excess hormones. If your current fibre intake is low then increase the fibre rich foods gradually. Make sure you chew your food properly.

Move well

There is a whole phase coming up on movement however remember here that inactivity can lead to, amongst other things, a sluggish bowel resulting in a build-up of toxins and possibly constipation. Movement will stimulate the internal organs to get things moving. All movement is wonderful although there are several yoga postures that are known to stimulate the liver.

Alongside these basics, abdominal massage has been shown to be a safe and effective way to stimulate bowel movement and adopting a good toileting position can improve things too. Ideally sit with your knees higher than your hips and lean forward, lightly resting your elbows on your knees. You can buy a 'squatty potty' to help you achieve this position though placing a rolled-up bath towel or a spare toilet roll under each foot will have the same effect.

Our gut is intricately linked to the brain and our emotions. Poor gut health can cause brain fog whilst the bowels respond to emotional stress in their own way. Constipation or diarrhoea can present in times of stress, so please notice the connection and manage the stress. Take the action and address the root cause rather than accept or normalise the symptoms.

I have, as I said I would, only skimmed the surface of gut health in this phase. But there is one more thing I need to tell you before we move on though. Inflammation in the gut and imbalance in microbiome can fragment sleep. The catch with this is that sleep enriches the gut microbiome. Fortunately, the conversation for improving your sleep is where we are heading next.

Wellness wisdom from phase two

Eliminate diet or low-fat foods and add in more real food and good fats, though watch your serving size.

Make it a mission to eat more vegetables than fruit, especially cooked cruciferous veggie such as broccoli, cauliflower, cabbage, brussel sprouts and kale.

Drink an extra glass of water today and continue to drink more until you are drinking two to three litres of water every day. If you drink several cups of tea or coffee a day, have a glass a water while the kettle is boiling or have a glass of water after every cup of tea or coffee as a water 'chaser'.

Phase three

Prioritise your sleep

Our bodies NEED restorative sleep to repair, to reset our blood sugar levels, re-balance our hormones and, without going too deep, to clear the build-up of plaque in the brain that impacts our cognitive health.

So many people normalise poor sleep, convinced that they just 'don't sleep well'.

Of course, there can be factors creating disruptive sleep including night feeds, young children, pets or snoring partners. However, although common, it is NOT normal to 'not sleep well'.

If you wake up every night at 2am with your brain in overdrive or regularly at 4am without reason or you feel wide awake the second your head hits the pillow despite feeling tired when you got into bed, then your body is asking for something. It needs your attention in the form of nourishment, movement, stress management or self-care.

The 2am wake up is often a sign of adrenal imbalance, caused by elevated stress, as we found out in phase one.

The 4am wake up is usually down to your blood sugar and an imbalance which can be caused by skipping meals, too much sugar or alcohol or a change in your body's metabolism and how it stores and uses insulin.

Lack of sleep day after day which easily runs into week after week and month after month could be affecting your cognitive health, fat loss goals and hormones, amongst other things.

Sometimes poor sleep is the result of a lack of routine, or unhelpful habits that we create and repeat over time without recognising their impact. If this is the case, going back to basics is all it takes to optimise your sleep.

Think of a child's bedtime routine, usually they go to bed at the same time every night having had dinner a good few hours earlier. They maybe have a bath and a warm drink before a bedtime story, all snuggled up in bed in their calm, dimly lit, cool room. Often they will have spent some time playing outside during the day and so once they have dropped off they tend to sleep through, waking up the next morning refreshed and full of energy.

As an adult the story is usually very different. The time of going to bed often varies, electronic devices are usually checked just before lights out and are then put on the bedside table for our morning alarm call. Dinner is eaten late or at irregular times, the large glass of wine is finished just before you go to bed and you might just watch one episode of your favourite Netflix series in bed on your tablet…. or maybe two, one more episode won't hurt!

Creating a quality evening routine that calms the brain and the body will help to bring balance to the sympathetic and parasympatric nervous system. This will actively lower your stress levels and prepare your body for restorative sleep and also supports repair of your adrenals that I spoke about in phase one.

As with the morning routine, an evening routine doesn't need to be a long and complicated practice, but how you end the day is as important as how well you start it, which means it needs a checklist!

Use the checklist on the following pages to create or re-introduce some new or different habits that will support your sleep quality and therefore improve the fundamentals that are compromised by poor sleep. You will recognise some of the strategies from the morning routine checklist.

I'm sure you're tired of reading that there is no 'one size fits all' and, of course, that applies to sleep hygiene too but use the following checklist as a guide to find the best routine for YOU. As with the morning routine, you don't have to do everything listed or spend an hour on each one. Simply spending 10 minutes on a couple of these activities (or similar) will be another game changer.

You may need to try or expand on a few of the following suggestions before you find the ones that work for you and your sleep improves. Or it may be that your sleep improves whilst you are addressing another of the areas of your wellbeing in this guide. Complete wellbeing is like a jigsaw, it doesn't matter which piece you start with, it will connect with another one. Nothing works in isolation, a change to one area can positively impact several other areas.

One more, possibly random but very important, thing you should bear in mind is that as the brain starts to calm, the door to the sub-conscious is open so beware of what you listen to / hear in the final 20 minutes before you sleep. It will have an impact without you even realising.

Evening routine activities

Eliminate blue screen light

The blue light emitted from computer screens, phones and tablets wakes up the brain and suppresses melatonin, the hormone needed to sleep. Set a curfew, at least an hour before you go to bed, and at that time, turn off electronic devices and engage in a brain calming activity instead. Maybe read a book (an actual book not a kindle), try journaling, colouring or take a warm bath.

Magnesium or epsom salt bath

I'll talk more about magnesium in a moment but here it's important to emphasise that it is a vital mineral for, amongst other things, sleep. Magnesium can be found in whole grains, nuts seeds, chickpeas, lentils, dark green leafy vegetables and dark chocolate but also in varying forms of supplement, including magnesium flakes (magnesium chloride) or espom salts (magnesium sulphate).

Our skin is our biggest organ and what we put on it is absorbed by it. Therefore, soaking for 20 minutes in a magnesium flake or epsom salt bath can not only calm the brain and body but also enhance your magnesium levels. It can also soothe skin conditions like eczema, acne, psoriasis and dermatitis, improve skin hydration and relieve joint pain or muscle aches.

If you are not a bath person you can still benefit from magnesium flakes or epsom salts by simply soaking your feet in a bowl of them or adding them to a foot bath. This, however, isn't recommended for people with diabetes.

Brain dumping or planning tomorrow

In the same way that journaling in the morning helps to organise your thoughts, worries and dreams, a brain dump before bed lightens the load you are carrying in your mind which allows the brain to calm down in preparation for sleep.

So many of us get to the end of the day replaying conversations we've had, worrying about what we said or didn't say. We often mentally beat ourselves up for the things we didn't do and are already thinking about all the things we must do tomorrow.

Getting those thoughts from the day and tasks for tomorrow out of our head eliminates the busyness in the brain and brings calm which is the key.

How often have you woken up in the night thinking of something you must remember to do tomorrow and then had more restless sleep whilst you continued to think about it, trying not to forget by the morning? Planning for tomorrow should prevent this.

Journalling, writing or colouring

This is slightly different to the brain dump I have just mentioned and is more about providing you with a form of escape as maybe you start to pen your own story or future vision. There are some journaling prompts in the extra recourses section at the back.

If writing or journaling aren't for you then grab some crayons or pens and spend 10 minutes colouring in or just doodling.

Meditating or breathing practice

As this does in the morning routine, a short, intentional breath practice before bed will focus your attention and reduce busy thoughts and chatter in the brain to prepare it for restful sleep.

Reading

A few pages or a short chapter is all you need to reap the benefits. A research study carried out by cognitive neuropsychologist Dr David Lewis showed that after only six minutes of reading a book, stress levels were reduced by 68%.

It doesn't matter what you chose to read, whether it's fiction, personal development or an autobiography, but please pick up a book every day and make it a real book with paper pages if you can.

There are so many more benefits of reading, as well as reducing your cortisol levels, but I just want to share this one with you because I believe there needs to be more conversation around cognitive health. As we age our memory and brain function deteriorate but studies have found that reading regularly increases your brain power, keeping your mind sharp and slowing down this mental decline.

Airplane mode

Having electronics in the bedroom at night can disturb restful sleep. Phone notifications may go off and wake you. Even if on silent, the light of the phone when they come through can cause you to stir if you are very light sensitive.

If you are currently accustomed to the 2am or 4am wake up and your phone is by your side you may be tempted to check it, as you can't sleep anyway. There is also the risk of checking your social media and emails just once more before you go to sleep which undoes the good of the blue screen curfew previously mentioned.

So many of us rely on our phone alarm clock and if that is you and you really don't want to get an old school alarm clock then please turn your phone to airplane mode when you go to bed. Your alarm will still work even with this setting on. I would also encourage you to put your phone on the other side of the room, not only to remove the temptation to check it if you wake in the night, but also to make you get out of bed the first time your alarm goes off. This will support your morning routine and stress management strategies. If you have to get out of bed to switch it off then you are less likely to snooze your alarm or switch it off and scroll through your phone for half an hour before you get up, preventing the unnecessary release of cortisol. Getting up first time will also give you the time to complete your morning routine.

Evening routine checklist

☐ Eliminate blue screen light

🛁 Magnesium or epsom salt bath

✏️ Brain dumping or planning tomorrow

📚 Journalling, writing or colouring

🫁 Meditating or breathing practice

📖 Reading

📶 Airplane mode

Date / day started:

Evening routine checklist

📱	Eliminate blue screen light
🛁	Magnesium or epsom salt bath
✏️	Brain dumping or planning tomorrow
📚	Journalling, writing or colouring
🫁	Meditating or breathing practice
📖	Reading
📡	Airplane mode

Date / day started:

Evening routine checklist

Eliminate blue screen light

Magnesium or epsom salt bath

Brain dumping or planning tomorrow

Journalling, writing or colouring

Meditating or breathing practice

Reading

Airplane mode

Date / day started:

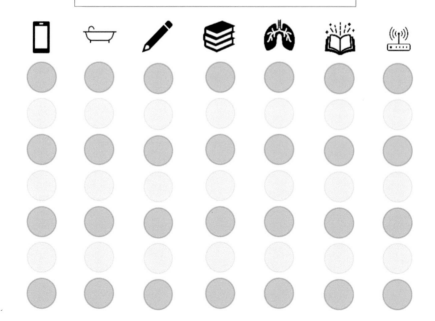

Evening routine checklist

📱 Eliminate blue screen light

🛁 Magnesium or epsom salt bath

✏️ Brain dumping or planning tomorrow

📚 Journalling, writing or colouring

🫁 Meditating or breathing practice

📖 Reading

📡 Airplane mode

Date / day started:

📱	🛁	✏️	📚	🫁	📖	📡
⚪	⚪	⚪	⚪	⚪	⚪	⚪
⚪	⚪	⚪	⚪	⚪	⚪	⚪
⚪	⚪	⚪	⚪	⚪	⚪	⚪
⚪	⚪	⚪	⚪	⚪	⚪	⚪
⚪	⚪	⚪	⚪	⚪	⚪	⚪
⚪	⚪	⚪	⚪	⚪	⚪	⚪
⚪	⚪	⚪	⚪	⚪	⚪	⚪

Evening routine checklist

- Eliminate blue screen light
- Magnesium or epsom salt bath
- Brain dumping or planning tomorrow
- Journalling, writing or colouring
- Meditating or breathing practice
- Reading
- Airplane mode

Date / day started:

Evening routine checklist

📱   Eliminate blue screen light

🛁   Magnesium or epsom salt bath

✏️   Brain dumping or planning tomorrow

📚   Journalling, writing or colouring

🫁   Meditating or breathing practice

📖   Reading

📶   Airplane mode

Date / day started:

"A well-spent day brings happy sleep"

Leonardo da Vinci

Alongside creating a quality evening routine, you also need to consider your sleeping environment as this has a huge impact on restful sleep. Keep your bedroom cool and the lights low. If you are sensitive to light, use blackout blinds at the windows and perhaps an eye mask. The latter might not look sexy but as the JoJo Jensen quote says "without enough sleep, we all become tall two-year-olds," which I'm sure you'll agree is a worse look!

Ensure that you go to bed and wake at the same time every-day. Short sleeps during the week and binge sleeping on the weekend does not equate to quality sleep.

If you struggle to fall asleep or wake up during the night and then can't sleep for more than 20 minutes, get out of bed for a short time. We are creatures of habit and if you remain in bed awake you teach yourself that being in the bedroom means being alert and awake, which will, of course, affect your sleep quality further. Although you may get up, avoid checking your electronic device or putting on the tv. Instead, grab a book, with real pages, or a magazine, your journal or even a colouring book. Have a warm un-caffeinated drink (herbal tea), maybe listen to a guided meditation and when you start to feel sleepy again, go back to bed. Train your body that bed is for sleep (and intimate shenanigans).

As I said at the beginning of this phase, a lack of routine is only *sometimes* the cause of poor sleep. If you are waking up at 2am or 4am then start before the start and implement the strategies to reduce your stress or balance your blood sugar. Reduce your caffeine and alcohol intake. These are stimulants which can both cause a spike in blood sugar so reduce your evening consumption, or avoid totally for 4-6 hours before bed. Avoid skipping meals and ensure you are eating quality protein at every meal. You could also add in a light protein snack before bed if you are seeing 4am on the alarm clock every morning!

As well as improving and enriching your evening routine, reducing stress and balancing your blood sugar, the most important, and probably easiest, thing you can do to improve your sleep is go outside… first thing in the morning!

Daylight exposure within 20 minutes of waking re-sets the circadian rhythm (the internal sleep / wake cycle) and your hormones. Please don't feel disheartened that this is 'another' thing you must do though. Incorporate it into your new morning routine. Eat your breakfast in the garden, take your book or journal and glass of water outside, walk around the block, workout on the patio - just spend 5 minutes in your PJ's and dressing gown breathing or mediating but absorbing the natural daylight into the eyes for a re-set at the same time.

I mentioned in phase two, the importance of magnesium for repairing the gut, but it is also a key supplement for sleep. Magnesium can be found in whole grains, nuts seeds, dark green leafy vegetables and dark chocolate.

There are hundreds of magnesium supplements available and this may be one of the minerals that you chose to supplement, but again please do your research. Chose a quality one and the best form of this mineral for you. Magnesium Citrate is the most common magnesium formulation. It is easily absorbed and good for a sluggish bowel, making it ideal if you do suffer with constipation but less so if you have an already loose stool. If this is the case you should firstly monitor your fibre intake and secondly consider and research an alternative form, such as Magnesium Malate which is also well absorbed, but may have less of a laxative effect. In addition, it may also improve fatigue symptoms and muscular pain.

Remember how I said in the introduction that any problematic hormonal symptoms you are experiencing are showing up for a reason? That these symptoms are your body's way of telling you that it is out of balance and lacking in something that it needs? Fragmented sleep can be a sign of declining progesterone, one of the main sex hormones. I'll share more about this in the next phase BUT if your sleep becomes disrupted towards day 23/24 of your cycle (if you are still menstruating) it does not mean it is 'just your age' or 'just your hormones' and there is nothing you can do. Please do not ever just normalise poor sleep.

Wellness wisdom from phase three

Start an evening routine tonight. Complete at least one or two of the activities on the evening routine checklist.

Set the intention to get outside first thing tomorrow morning. Set your alarm five minutes earlier if you need to. Take your morning coffee or breakfast outside or stand by the back door while the kettle is boiling. Don't be deterred by the weather, wrap yourself in a blanket if needs be, but reset your sleep/wake cycle as soon as you can after waking.

Instead of scrolling through your phone before bed tonight and reading the news or social media updates, pick up a book and read a chapter of that instead.

Phase four

<u>Nurturing happy hormones</u>

As I shared way back in the introduction, hormones influence EVERYTHING that happens in your body - your mood, sleep, weight and energy. I hope by now you realise that you can take action to rewrite your own health and wellbeing story and take control of your hormones, rather than being controlled by them. Particularly during those years when you might not even be thinking about your hormones specifically but just know that you're exhausted, frustrated and the diets and intense workouts you are doing are having absolutely no effect.

Nobody knows your body like you do but sometimes we just become too busy to notice the changes or the mild symptoms we experience until they become problematic and need deeper attention. I therefore encourage you to track your cycle daily. It is only by paying close attention to yourself and knowing WHAT you feel, HOW you feel it and WHEN you feel it that you can recognise what your body needs from you and when.

On the following pages you will find my hormone symptom tracker. There will likely be things on this checklist that you've not previously given much thought to or recognised. It is when we start to really pay attention, that we can identify a connection, absence or irregularity and this is when the right strategies for managing the symptom can be implemented.

The symptom tracker I am sharing allows you to record your period but if you are no longer menstruating, I still encourage you to use it. Your body continues to produce hormones post-menopause so you may still experience the symptoms listed despite not having a period. Also, symptoms don't always present because of your sex hormones, there can be other factors that cause them and is why the tracker is important.

A final thing on the tracker and normalising symptoms. If you are still menstruating, either regularly or irregularly, it is normal to experience some MILD grumpiness, fatigue and cramps before your period. Anything beyond that can be a red flag for a greater health concern. Any pelvic or abdominal PAIN, VERY heavy, VERY light or irregular bleeds, chronic yeast infections or unexplained digestive issues should be investigated. These are NOT normal symptoms.

Hormone symptom tracker

Use this key to track your symptoms. Only by paying close attention to yourself and knowing WHAT you feel, HOW you feel and WHEN you feel it can you recognise what your body needs from you and when.

None O   Mild -   Moderate x   Severe /

Abdominal PAIN																		
Acne																		
Anxiety																		
Backache																		
Bladder PAIN																		
Bloating																		
Breast Tenderness																		
Constipation																		
Cramps																		
Crying Spells / Sadness																		
Diarrhoea																		
Difficulty Concentrating																		
Dizziness																		
Fatigue																		
Flatulence																		
Food Cravings																		
Headache / Migraine																		
Heavy Bleed																		
Hot Flushes																		
Irritability																		
Libido (Decreased)																		
Libido (Increased)																		
Light Bleed																		
Moody																		
Muscle Aches or Pains																		
Nausea																		
Pelvic PAIN																		
Sleep (Decreased)																		
Sleep (Increased)																		
Yeast Infection																		

Hormone symptom tracker

Use this key to track your symptoms. Only by paying close attention to yourself and knowing WHAT you feel, HOW you feel and WHEN you feel it can you recognise what your body needs from you and when.

None O   Mild -   Moderate x   Severe /

Abdominal PAIN																
Acne																
Anxiety																
Backache																
Bladder PAIN																
Bloating																
Breast Tenderness																
Constipation																
Cramps																
Crying Spells / Sadness																
Diarrhoea																
Difficulty Concentrating																
Dizziness																
Fatigue																
Flatulence																
Food Cravings																
Headache / Migraine																
Heavy Bleed																
Hot Flushes																
Irritability																
Libido (Decreased)																
Libido (Increased)																
Light Bleed																
Moody																
Muscle Aches or Pains																
Nausea																
Pelvic PAIN																
Sleep (Decreased)																
Sleep (Increased)																
Yeast Infection																

Hormone symptom tracker

Use this key to track your symptoms. Only by paying close attention to yourself and knowing WHAT you feel, HOW you feel and WHEN you feel it can you recognise what your body needs from you and when.

None O   Mild -   Moderate x   Severe /

Abdominal PAIN																
Acne																
Anxiety																
Backache																
Bladder PAIN																
Bloating																
Breast Tenderness																
Constipation																
Cramps																
Crying Spells / Sadness																
Diarrhoea																
Difficulty Concentrating																
Dizziness																
Fatigue																
Flatulence																
Food Cravings																
Headache / Migraine																
Heavy Bleed																
Hot Flushes																
Irritability																
Libido (Decreased)																
Libido (Increased)																
Light Bleed																
Moody																
Muscle Aches or Pains																
Nausea																
Pelvic PAIN																
Sleep (Decreased)																
Sleep (Increased)																
Yeast Infection																

Hormone symptom tracker

Use this key to track your symptoms. Only by paying close attention to yourself and knowing WHAT you feel, HOW you feel and WHEN you feel it can you recognise what your body needs from you and when.

None O   Mild -   Moderate x   Severe /

Abdominal PAIN																
Acne																
Anxiety																
Backache																
Bladder PAIN																
Bloating																
Breast Tenderness																
Constipation																
Cramps																
Crying Spells / Sadness																
Diarrhoea																
Difficulty Concentrating																
Dizziness																
Fatigue																
Flatulence																
Food Cravings																
Headache / Migraine																
Heavy Bleed																
Hot Flushes																
Irritability																
Libido (Decreased)																
Libido (Increased)																
Light Bleed																
Moody																
Muscle Aches or Pains																
Nausea																
Pelvic PAIN																
Sleep (Decreased)																
Sleep (Increased)																
Yeast Infection																

Hormone symptom tracker

Use this key to track your symptoms. Only by paying close attention to yourself and knowing WHAT you feel, HOW you feel and WHEN you feel it can you recognise what your body needs from you and when.

None O   Mild -   Moderate x   Severe /

Abdominal PAIN															
Acne															
Anxiety															
Backache															
Bladder PAIN															
Bloating															
Breast Tenderness															
Constipation															
Cramps															
Crying Spells / Sadness															
Diarrhoea															
Difficulty Concentrating															
Dizziness															
Fatigue															
Flatulence															
Food Cravings															
Headache / Migraine															
Heavy Bleed															
Hot Flushes															
Irritability															
Libido (Decreased)															
Libido (Increased)															
Light Bleed															
Moody															
Muscle Aches or Pains															
Nausea															
Pelvic PAIN															
Sleep (Decreased)															
Sleep (Increased)															
Yeast Infection															

Hormone symptom tracker

Use this key to track your symptoms. Only by paying close attention to yourself and knowing WHAT you feel, HOW you feel and WHEN you feel it can you recognise what your body needs from you and when.

None O   Mild -   Moderate x   Severe /

Abdominal PAIN																	
Acne																	
Anxiety																	
Backache																	
Bladder PAIN																	
Bloating																	
Breast Tenderness																	
Constipation																	
Cramps																	
Crying Spells / Sadness																	
Diarrhoea																	
Difficulty Concentrating																	
Dizziness																	
Fatigue																	
Flatulence																	
Food Cravings																	
Headache / Migraine																	
Heavy Bleed																	
Hot Flushes																	
Irritability																	
Libido (Decreased)																	
Libido (Increased)																	
Light Bleed																	
Moody																	
Muscle Aches or Pains																	
Nausea																	
Pelvic PAIN																	
Sleep (Decreased)																	
Sleep (Increased)																	
Yeast Infection																	

"It's not your hormones, it's their environment"

Cheryl Burdette

Any wellbeing niggles you might be experiencing as a result of your hormones, including poor sleep, inch loss resistance and low energy, might not necessarily be because your hormones are declining. For me, stress and gut health cause the greatest hormonal disruption and their own symptoms which may be mistaken for hormonal symptoms, such as brain fog, low mood and fragmented sleep. You may find by implementing the strategies that I have already suggested in phases one and two, your symptom tracker symbols change.

Of course there will come a time when your hormones themselves will begin their natural decline but that doesn't mean you have to, or will experience troublesome symptoms though. Remember that your adrenals will pick up the slack as your ovaries slow down so doing the work and supporting your adrenals BEFORE they are called on will help hugely. Also know that no one will experience the same transition through the peri to post menopause years. Some will sail through whilst others may need additional support and medication but that is a deeper and more individual conversation that I would recommend you have with a hormone specialist if, and when, the time comes. That said I feel that there is some essential information every woman should know about hormones.

As with everything else I have shared up to this point the following information is general. These are the core facts about the some of the key hormones that once you know might alter how you nourish your body and support your cycle. Remember the more we know the better we do.

The facts about hormones

All hormones work together. So if one is out of balance there will be a cascade of unbalance though the entire endocrine system, which in turn can cause hormonal symptoms and wellbeing niggles.

- Puberty can last up to seven years.
- The average age for women to go through the menopause is 52.

- The peri-menopause can last for between seven and fifteen years.
- Symptoms don't always stop post menopause.
- The menstrual cycle, which is counted from the first day of one period to the first day of the next, varies from woman to woman.
- The average cycle is 28 days.
- Cycles that are longer or shorter than this, from 21 to 35 days, are normal.
- The main sex hormones continually fluctuate during your cycle and all have a different role.

The main sex hormones

The main sex hormones - estrogen, progesterone and testosterone - are derived from fat meaning that low fat diets can be problematic for hormonal health. Heart health, bone health and pelvic health can be effected by the decline of estrogen, exercise can support all of these and I'll be sharing more about purposeful movement in the next phase.

ESTROGEN

- The fiery hormone.
- **Mild** moodiness is expected when levels are low BUT anything beyond that is an indication that something isn't right. As is excessive fatigue and severe stomach pain.

TESTOSTERONE

- The hormone of sex and motivation.
- At the beginning your cycle estrogen and testosterone are most dominant so after day five of your period you should be starting to think about sex and feel more confident and motivated.

After ovulation around day 14, **progesterone** becomes more dominant.

PROGESTERONE

- The anti-depressant and sleep supportive hormone.
- If you experience anxiety towards the end of your cycle (around day 23) or your sleep is fragmented, it's a sign that progesterone levels may be low.
- Shorter cycles are often a sign that the body is not producing enough progestogen.

Estrogen and progesterone work together. Imagine estrogen is growing grass and progesterone is the mower. If these two hormones fall out of balance with each other there be an effect on all the other hormones but some of the most common troublesome symptoms are likely to show up.

There are chemicals in our skincare, beauty products, candles, room fragrances and cleaning products that can mimic our own estrogen, causing a potential estrogen dominance and therefore imbalance with progesterone. Start to check what is really in the products you use and eliminate anything that could be hormonally disruptive and support your liver to remove any excess hormones from the body.

VITAMIN D

- Vitamin D is a hormone and every cell in the body has vitamin D receptors.
- Like the main sex hormones, vitamin D is a fat-derived vitamin so the fat free, low fat, fad diets are not helpful. Please step away from them and **just** eat real food.
- Vitamin D is found in a small number of foods including oily fish, liver, egg yolks, mushrooms though it is generally made from sunshine. Most of us should be able to get sufficient exposure to the sun without risking damage.
- Vitamin D is critical to bone health and the immune system.
- Obesity and high alcohol consumption suppress vitamin D levels.
- Vitamin D can't be absorbed without sufficient K2.

HUMAN GROWTH HORMONE (hGH)

- The hormone of youth that plays a key role in the switch that takes you from storing to burning fat.
- After the age of 30, our hGH levels decline at about 12 to 15% per decade and the visible signs of aging start to show.
- Exercise is one of the most effective ways to raise your hGH levels.

The thyroid is a phase, if not a book, of its own but because so many women, unknowingly, struggle with their thyroid, brushing off or normalising the symptoms that they are experiencing, I want to share the most important thyroid information with you before we move on.

The thyroid is the queen of the endocrine system, the thermostat for our body, turning up or down our metabolic rate, alertness and temperature. Although the thyroid gland is in the neck, the thyroid hormone is converted into the strongest form of itself in peripheral tissues including your gut, liver and kidneys.

If the gut is inflamed, or the nutrients needed to convert the thyroid are deficient then that process is compromised. Therefore, supporting your gut health and reducing inflammation in the gut is vital for your thyroid. In return, the thyroid hormones are needed for gut function which is why low thyroid can have symptoms of constipation or bloating, amongst others. Too much stress will also supress the conversion process.

GPs are generally quite happy to run a thyroid test, but they tend to only measure two of the thyroid markers (TSH & Free T4). They rarely measure your active thyroid (T3) which is the one that does all the work. The reference ranges for 'normal' on these tests do also widely vary. You may have a test which comes back with a 'normal' result even though you know there is something amiss. In response your GP will likely be unconcerned and suggest either another reason for your symptoms or to test again at a later date. I have worked with clients who have improved normal or borderline underactive readings by using the strategies I have recommended in the previous phases.

If you are troubled by your own 'normal' thyroid reading then please re-visit phase one and two and implement the suggestions, follow up with your GP or investigate further with a hormone specialist.

Wellness wisdom for phase four

Start to use the symptom tracker in this phase, even if you are no longer menstruating.

Check the ingredients in the skincare and household products you use.

Recognise any symptoms you are experiencing and identify the cause. Do not normalise them as 'just your age' or 'just your hormones'.

Phase five

<u>Exercise well not more</u>

It is far too common for time poor and exhausted women to be punishing their beautiful bodies with intense workouts. Working out longer and harder to crush calories, earn the wine and chocolate or try and shift the mid-section weight gain they may have started to notice.

But the days of eat less, move more are long gone.

It is time to look at a whole-body approach and, for me, that means working out well NOT more! Exercising to nourish our mind and body, within the time and energy we have and to consider our heart health, bone health, pelvic health, cognitive health and, now we know about the importance of it, our adrenal health.

All movement is wonderful but we need to add a variety of training styles into our workouts. This doesn't mean that you need to spend hours at a time in a gym, using every piece of cardio equipment. In fact, depending on the other markers we have already spoken about, that could do more harm than good.

Let's take it back to the hormones for a second. Whilst this guide is about the years before the peri to post menopause life phase, I want to share with you some of the deeper facts about hormonal decline because prevention is vital for some of the after-effects.

Whilst estrogen is the fiery hormone it has over 400 other functions including maintaining the structure and function of the muscle, tendon and ligament tissue. When it declines the tendons feel it. One in four women in their 50's develop hip and rotator cuff issues. Frozen shoulder and plantar fasciitis are also very common in peri and menopausal women.

Our bone health is reliant on estrogen, alongside optimum nutrient absorption. We can lose as much as 20% of our bone density in the first few years of menopause. It is also the cardio protective hormone. Heart disease is the biggest cause of death in women, killing more than twice as many women as breast cancer in the UK every year.

All of these conditions are, however, responsive to the **right type** of exercise and a few other elements because of course it is not going to just be about movement. We need to ensure that our connective tissue doesn't dry out, which we can do simply by staying hydrated and drinking enough water every day. As I shared in phase two, aim to drink 2 – 3 litres of water every day. Tea (unless herbal) and coffee do not count towards your water total and PLEASE don't avoid drinking enough water through fear of leakage.

To support our bone health we need to add in regular 'bone loading' movement. You can't bank bone: bones are alive and their re-modelling is a lifelong process. It is vital to do the work to keep your bones strong by moving well and consistently and absorbing the right nutrients and vitamins (vitamin D and K2 are vital for calcium absorption), as well as reducing exposure to calcium 'thieves'. Calcium 'thieves' include, amongst many other things, caffeine, alcohol and of course stress (hello again phase one!).

Movement for your bone health requires a combination of weight-bearing exercise with impact and, because nothing works in isolation, muscle strengthening exercise. Please don't be put off by the impact bit. This doesn't mean that you need to start running. In fact, running alone is not a great bone-strengthening activity. Low level jumping, skipping and hopping are all amazing. Even brisk walking, marching, stair climbing and stamping your feet will work your bones. You can, of course, add in high level or star jumps but please consider your pelvic floor and ensure that your movement is pelvic floor safe for you. It is never too late to support your bones. Poor bone density does not have to mean poor bone quality.

For me, resistance training is an essential form of movement for every woman. That can be lifting your own body weight, using resistance machines or a resistance band or, my absolute favourite, lifting free weights (dumbbells). Resistance training is a game changer for our body shape, strength and bone health. So many women worry that if they lift heavy weights they will bulk up but we don't have enough testosterone, even before levels start to decline, for that to happen. Lifting weights will instead 'rev up' your metabolism in a way that causes your body to continue to burn fat at rest. This just doesn't happen from cardio training. Therefore if inch loss is your goal, I strongly encourage you to start lifting weights.

Head to my website www.victoriajones.co.uk for details of my online 'Weights for Women' programme. Lifting weights is also less stressful on the body ,which starts the next part of the move well conversation.

"I will not let
age change me.
I will change
the way I age"

Heather Hayes

I shared in phase one that, prehistorically, the greatest danger to trigger the stress response would have been a sabre tooth tiger. When you are working out hard, spending an hour or more completing intense cardio workouts, your brain doesn't know that you're not being chased by that tiger so to keep you safe it sends the signal to the adrenals to release the stress hormone, cortisol.

Of course, we do need to get out of breath and hot and sweaty to protect our heart health and to stimulate the production of the human growth hormone. However, short bursts of intensity are much more beneficial than long cardio sessions.

That is not to say that if you want run long distances or join a high impact class every day that you shouldn't. Just add in an adequate amount of rest and recovery. Ensure you are calming and supporting the adrenals. If you are regularly completing long or hight impact cardio workouts you need to consider:

- What time you go to bed?
- How much daylight exposure are you getting?
- How much time do you spend connecting with friends?
- How much water are you drinking?
- What are you eating? Are you including sufficient protein, vitamins and minerals?

Your body won't be able to keep up with high demand workouts whilst spinning the home, family, business and life plates without some wellbeing niggle presenting itself if the other considerations aren't in place.

Please don't feel overwhelmed by this phase and the different workout styles your body needs, or worry about how you are going to fit it in to an already busy schedule. I assure you that little, often, varied and purposeful is the best strategy to exercising. It really is about moving well NOT more. Workouts honestly only need to be between 10 – 40 minutes for maximum benefit. Throughout a week include some metabolic training and some restorative and strength workouts. As with everything I've shared, there will be a crossover of benefits from each of these workout styles including improving foot proprioception to keep the feet alive and supporting neuroplasticity and neurogenesis to keep the brain cells sharp.

Metabolic training is a wellbeing gift, it is a workout strategy where you work in short, intense periods. The intensity is the key but that doesn't mean high impact. The short burst of movement need to hit these four markers:

1. Get you hot
2. Get you sweaty
3. Make you out of breath
4. Cause a burn in the muscles

Testosterone and the human growth hormone both increase in production as your exercise intensity increases and you hit these markers. Don't worry though, you still won't produce enough testosterone to bulk up.

One final thing about these markers is that feeling the burn does not mean stop. That is the sign to keep going because that is where the changes happen and your body responds. You can complete an effective metabolic style workout in a very short time and I would encourage that you complete one two or three times per week.

I have shared how the structure and function of the muscle, tendon and ligament tissue alters as our bodies change, however we live in a predominantly forward-facing world which is impacting our posture and alignment. Poor posture can cause stiffness, discomfort and pain through our back, neck and shoulders. It can aggravate any arthritis you may suffer with and also lead to much deeper health complications. Poor posture also affects your mood, digestion and sleep.

Over time the glutes will also weaken partially because of the length of time we sit, partially because of poor posture and partially because of the decline in estrogen. The weakening of the glutes can affect our pelvic, hip and knee health and breath function so it is vital that we add in movement for our core strength, posture and alignment. This is usually where the restorative workouts, such as yoga and pilates will be effective.

These workout styles will also support the repair of your adrenals and are a great stress management exercise. I would also encourage you to add in some glute activation exercises, either through one of the workout styles already mentioned or as a specific workout. Head over to www.victoriajones.co.uk/reignite-resources and you'll find a short metabolic, Fitness Pilates, glute activation and weights workout that you can try.

Movement can increase your metabolism, help to get nutrients to your cells, stimulate your vital organs to help eliminate toxins and activate hormone production. Whilst I've shared the general styles of workout we need to incorporate for the different areas of our wellbeing you need to find the exact form that suits YOU! Your movement needs to bring you joy and energise you, not exhaust you. A dance class might light you up much more than a short metabolic workout and will hit most, if not all depending on the style, of the same markers as well as load your bones.

Of course it's not only the movement. Yes, increase your daily movement and make it purposeful and joyful but also make sure that, alongside it, you are eating a nutrient dense and varied diet, adding in restorative self- care activities, managing your stress and prioritising your sleep.

Because I know inch loss is a wellbeing goal for so many women and I've just shared how effective lifting weights is for fat burning I must finish this phase by sharing something very important with you.

So many of us are fixated on our weight and the numbers on the scales. When you start to do the work in this guide and calm and restore your adrenals, improve your sleep, balance your hormones to flick the switch from fat storing to fat burning and lift your weights, the stubborn weight gain that you tried to shift for years will melt away. However, the number on the scales might not reflect these changes.

Whilst it is commonly said that muscle is heavier than fat, a lb is a lb.

A lb of lead weighs the same as a lb of marshmallows, the mass is just different and this is the same for muscle and fat. When your muscle strength improves, because of the right movement, and your body fat reduces because of the new strategies you're implementing, there will be changes. But please don't rely on the scales to show you this change.

Instead, notice your clothes fitter better or your energy levels rising, that you look and feel good. These are all much more important than the number on the scale. What's more, nobody walks around with a set of scales showing people they meet how much they weigh. When you slim down, no one ever tells you that you look lighter! We shop based a dress size of inches not on scale weight so please don't use that as your health measure.

Wellness wisdom for phase five

Keep your workouts short, varied and purposeful.

When you feel a burn in your muscles keep going just a little bit longer.

Find movement that brings you joy.

Stop using the scales to measure your progress and success.

Final thoughts

Thank you for reading to this point I am so grateful and honoured you have chosen to read my guide. However, if you've only read through the pages so far, you now need to go back and start to implement the strategies.

Even if you know what to do or if this guide has just reminded of those things, use the checklists and complete the interactive pages. The few minutes it might take to action and complete the suggestions each day will have a hugely positive impact and in a very short space of time.

Do not underestimate the power of the small simple things. Achieving your health and wellness goals, hormonal balance, increased energy and improved sleep will not happen by adding in one big strategy. These changes will come from adding in the little strategies I've shared and, more importantly, repeating them regularly.

You may have to dig deep for motivation when you don't feel like doing the workout or turning off your phone at 8pm to go and have a soak in the bath. Scrolling through social media might feel so much more entertaining than reading a chapter of your book – in which case you need to change you book! When you don't feel like getting up to your alarm so you can complete your morning routine you will need to remind yourself that only YOU can protect your wellbeing and if nothing changes, nothing will improve and instead it will get progressively worse.

Of course, the strategies in this guide are very broad and for information only. If you need deeper guidance or personalised support then please consult the best professional for you.

If you are concerned about your hormones after using the symptom tracker in phase four then speak to a hormone specialist who can test your hormones and make recommendations based on your specific results. If after becoming your own diet detective, you sense you might need additional nutrition input, please arrange a consultation with an Association for Nutrition registered nutritionist (UKVRN), dietitian or qualified functional medicine practitioner to investigate gut microbiome testing. If, after identifying your stresses you feel there is something emotional that is too heavy for you to manage on your own then consider some talking therapy, coaching or holistic healing. If you would like support or accountability to build new habits based on the strategies I've shared or, if you would love to keep the conversations I've started here going, then please join me in my Women's Wellbeing Association, an online platform with **ONE** mission:

To support, encourage and motivate women in every area of their wellbeing; physically, mentally and emotionally

You can find more details about the Women's Wellbeing Association on page 122.

There is so much I haven't told you yet. Perhaps that will be a story for another day, a sequel to this start point. Until then, I hope this guide has given you clarity and confidence to take control of your hormones and wellbeing. Remember, hormones control EVERYTHING in your body - your mood, sleep, weight and energy.

ALL hormones work together, if one is out of balance they will all be out of balance and that is when the hormonal symptoms and wellbeing niggles will show up. That doesn't mean you have to accept them. Whist they are common, they are NOT normal. It's not 'just your age' or 'just your hormones'. It is your body telling you that it is lacking in something that it needs. Deeper nourishment, movement or rest and relaxation, something to calm and nurture.

There is not a 'one size fits all' solution to hormonal imbalance or wellbeing, but everyone must apply a whole-body approach and apply the basics – drink water, just eat real food, add in more joy, stress management strategies and supportive movement. Don't forget to head over to www.victoriajones.co.uk/reignite-resources for the workouts.

You do not need to wait until symptoms show up to start to support your hormones or wellbeing.

You are a human BEING not a human doing and you must make time for YOU, for your own health, happiness and wellbeing.

Now is the time to value your health and wellbeing above all else. To put the work in and implement simple lifestyle strategies and small but effective habits that will make a real difference to how you feel. When you are energised and thriving you can give more to others.

Extra
Resources

Whilst I have shared both a morning and evening routine checklist I've also encouraged you to add in some other, hugely important, strategies each day which deserve their own checklist. The daily routine checklist that you will find on the following pages brings the key elements from all the phases together in one space. You might choose to use this checklist alongside the morning routine as some of the activities overlap or you might prefer to use it once your new morning habits have been created or re-instated.

The significance of using a checklist is the same. The brain loves it when we achieve something, or it can see us making progress. Every time you tick off an activity your brain will release the feel-good hormone, dopamine. The more you activate that dopamine release, the more your brain will want you to repeat the associated action or behaviour.

Daily routine checklist

Morning visualisation, meditation or breathwork

Because the stress hormone cortisol starts to naturally rise when we wake up, taking time first thing to complete a visualisation, mediation or to connect with your breath allows the natural elevation to begin to lower, restoring balance internally before you start the day.

Exercise

All movement is wonderful and our body is designed to move every day. Exercise doesn't need to be a high impact aerobics class, 60-minute gym session or 5k run. A daily 10-minute weights workout, yoga flow or walk around the block are often more effective. So many people unknowingly over exercise which can have a negative impact on inch loss goals, increase stress and disrupt hormones.

Daylight exposure

Daylight exposure is so important for regulating sleep patterns, lowering the stress hormone and for the production of vitamin D. Vitamin D is a hormone that is vital for so many functions from supporting strong and healthy bones and muscles to maintaining your immune system. Most of us should be able to get sufficient vitamin D from direct sunlight on the skin when outdoors without risking sun damage.

'Tiara Time'

This is YOU time… Time for the activities and hobbies that feed your soul with joy, that give your mind and body a break from the grind, being busy, looking after others, working, social media, learning. Again, this only needs to be ten minutes yet the difference it will have on you is immeasurable.

Drink water

To function properly, all the cells and organs in the body need water and yet so many of us don't drink enough. We should all be aiming to drink two – three litres of water every day. Tea (unless herbal) and coffee do not count towards your water total.

Eat greens

Dark green leafy veg is so important for so many areas of our wellbeing, including boosting our immune health, restoring balance in the gut, strengthening our bones, improving liver detoxification and supporting our hormones. An extra serving of greens a day has a powerful effect.

Daily routine checklist

🫁   Morning visualisation, meditation or breathwork

🏋   Exercise

☀   Daylight exposure

👑   'Tiara Time'

💧   Drink water

🥑   Eat greens

Date / day started:

🫁	🏋	☀	👑	💧	🥑
⚪	⚪	⚪	⚪	⚪	⚪
⚪	⚪	⚪	⚪	⚪	⚪
⚪	⚪	⚪	⚪	⚪	⚪
⚪	⚪	⚪	⚪	⚪	⚪
⚪	⚪	⚪	⚪	⚪	⚪
⚪	⚪	⚪	⚪	⚪	⚪
⚪	⚪	⚪	⚪	⚪	⚪

Daily routine checklist

🫁 Morning visualisation, meditation or breathwork

🏋 Exercise

☀ Daylight exposure

👑 'Tiara Time'

💧 Drink water

🥑 Eat greens

Date / day started:

🫁   🏋   ☀   👑   💧   🥑

Daily routine checklist

🫁   Morning visualisation, meditation or breathwork

🏋   Exercise

☀   Daylight exposure

👑   'Tiara Time'

💧   Drink water

🥑   Eat greens

Date / day started:

Daily routine checklist

🫁 Morning visualisation, meditation or breathwork

🏋 Exercise

☀ Daylight exposure

👑 'Tiara Time'

💧 Drink water

🥑 Eat greens

Date / day started:

🫁	🏋	☀	👑	💧	🥑
⬤	⬤	⬤	⬤	⬤	⬤
◯	◯	◯	◯	◯	◯
⬤	⬤	⬤	⬤	⬤	⬤
◯	◯	◯	◯	◯	◯
⬤	⬤	⬤	⬤	⬤	⬤
◯	◯	◯	◯	◯	◯
⬤	⬤	⬤	⬤	⬤	⬤

Daily routine checklist

🫁 Morning visualisation, meditation or breathwork

🏋 Exercise

☀ Daylight exposure

👑 'Tiara Time'

💧 Drink water

🥑 Eat greens

Date / day started:

🫁 🏋 ☀ 👑 💧 🥑

○ ○ ○ ○ ○ ○

○ ○ ○ ○ ○ ○

○ ○ ○ ○ ○ ○

○ ○ ○ ○ ○ ○

○ ○ ○ ○ ○ ○

○ ○ ○ ○ ○ ○

○ ○ ○ ○ ○ ○

Daily routine checklist

🫁 Morning visualisation, meditation or breathwork

🏋 Exercise

☀ Daylight exposure

👑 'Tiara Time'

💧 Drink water

🥑 Eat greens

Date / day started:

These last few pages include prompts to support both the morning and evening routine checklists and some other extra reflection activities. I recommend putting your thoughts onto paper to either bring you clarity, lighten the load you are carrying in your mind, or to organise your thoughts, worries and dreams.

Whether it is the tasks for the day ahead, thoughts from the day that is ending or tasks for tomorrow, once they are out of our head the busyness in the brain quietens. When you put your worries onto the paper, it is often easier to realise your next best step.

When you write your future plans, dreams or goals out or list the things you are grateful for, you activate the Reticular Activating System (RAS). This really is a whole other story for another day but, very briefly, the RAS is an automatic nerve mechanism in the brain. It's like a radar, taking instructions from your conscious mind and bringing only the information that is relevant to that instruction to your attention. All of this happens without you noticing, of course.

The best example I can give for how the RAS works is this. Have you noticed when you're considering buying a new car or you've just picked one up and then you see the same model everywhere? All of the time? This is your RAS at work. It's a powerful system for achieving your goals and again once they are written out your RAS will get to work to help you find the information, people and opportunities that will help you to achieve them.

On these final pages you will find space to put your thoughts. There are journaling prompts, spaces for gratitude and tasks and pages to dream and plan to activate the RAS. There is no right or wrong way to use these following pages. The key as with everything you've already read is simply to use them. There is also a 'Tiara Time' page, a space for you to list all the hobbies and activities that fill your mind, body and soul with happiness. Once they are written out you do need to create the time in your schedule to complete them.

Affirmations

An affirmation is a positive statement that you repeat to yourself, regularly throughout the day. You can say your affirmations out loud or silently in your head. You might like to write them as part of your morning routine from phase one and read them back several times during the day. You might prefer to create a screensaver for your mobile phone, so that you see your affirmation regularly. However you chose to use your affirmations, make sure the words you use in your statements:

√ FEEL exciting, happy, fulfilling and good.

√ Are in the present tense.

√ State the positive (affirm what you want, not what you DON'T want).

√ Are specific to the changes you want to see/feel/achieve.

Evidence-based studies confirm that affirmations can rewire our brains. Because the brain doesn't know what is real or not - which is why the stress response is triggered so often - we have the power within us to challenge and overturn negative and ineffective beliefs and thoughts.

Below are some powerful affirmations you might like to use. Or use the space on the next page to write your own.

I am enough.
I am making progress every day.
Today, I am brimming with energy and overflowing with joy.
My body is healthy, my mind is and calm.
Wonderful things come to me effortlessly and easily.
Money comes easily and frequently to me.

Affirmations

Write your own affirmations below. Write them in the present tense, as though you are experiencing your desires already and not in the future. Make sure you affirm what you WANT, not what you DON'T want. You do not have to fill out the whole page with affirmations but re-visit and update them as you notice the changes they bring.

'Tiara Time'

List the activities and hobbies that feed your soul with joy, that give your mind and body a break from the grind, being busy, looking after others, working, social media, learning. Schedule the things from this list into your calendar as 'Tiara Time'. You do not have to fill out the whole page with activities or implement them all immediately. There may be new hobbies you would like to try at a later date. You can add those here, along with any extra resources you might need for them (to activate the RAS) but PLEASE ensure that you are adding in other 'Tiara Time' activities to your schedule in the meantime

○ ....

○ ....

○ ....

○ ....

○ ....

○ ....

○ ....

○ ....

○ ....

○ ....

○ ....

○ ....

Goal setting

No matter what you're trying to achieve, setting goals is the most powerful thing you can do to make sure you get from where you are to where you want to be. Use the goal setting prompts over the following pages to help identify and define your top three goals and, importantly, the steps you need to take to achieve them.

You might choose to write the action steps in reverse order, so you think through all the details involved in success from the outset and identify any gaps where you'll need extra support or resources. You may decide to break your main goal into a few bigger steps and then each of these steps into smaller steps.

Depending on your goal the action steps you take could include:

> Researching or reading books or articles.
> Asking someone else for advice or guidance.
> Enrolling in a course to learn a new skill.
> Hiring a coach or joining a community, group or club.
> Blocking time out in your schedule to work on your action steps.

Revisit these goal setting pages often to tick off your progress and to make sure you're taking steps towards your dreams every single day. Remember to recognise what you HAVE done rather than focus on what is left to do.

Dare to dream because anything is possible, particularly when you write it down and activate your RAS (reticular activating system).

You can incorporate achieving your goals into your affirmations. For example:

> I am ready, willing, and able to achieve all my goals.
> I am equipped with all the tools I need to succeed.
> I focus my vision on my goals, aspirations, and dreams.

Notes

Goal Setting

Goal one:

....

....

....

....

Action steps: Done:

○

....

○

....

○

....

○

....

○

....

○

....

○

....

What resources are available to me?	What challenges might I face?	How will I overcome these challenges?

Notes

Goal Setting

Goal two:

....

....

....

....

Action steps: Done:

....

....

....

....

....

....

....

What resources are available to me?	What challenges might I face?	How will I overcome these challenges?

Notes

Goal Setting

Goal three:

....

....

....

....

Action steps: Done:

....

....

....

....

....

....

....

What resources are available to me?	What challenges might I face?	How will I overcome these challenges?

Gratitude

Gratitude is appreciating the good things in life, no matter how big or small. Taking time each day to be grateful can help to develop feelings of happiness and improve self-esteem.

Spend a few minutes each day to write down three to five good things that have happened or that you have achieved. They can be big things such as your home or car for example, or small things like enjoying a cup of coffee in the garden. It might be the people that you love, that make you smile or feel safe and supported. It might be something fabulous that happened during the day or the fact you overcame an obstacle.

Date:

1
....
2
....
3
....
4
....
5
....

Date:

1
....
2
....
3
....
4
....
5
....

Gratitude

Date:

1
....

2
....

3
....

4
....

5
....

Date:

1
....

2
....

3
....

4
....

5
....

Date:

1
....

2
....

3
....

4
....

5
....

Gratitude

Date:

1

2

3

4

5

Date:

1

2

3

4

5

Date:

1

2

3

4

5

Gratitude

Date:

1
....

2
....

3
....

4
....

5
....

Date:

1
....

2
....

3
....

4
....

5
....

Date:

1
....

2
....

3
....

4
....

5
....

Gratitude

Date:

1
....

2
....

3
....

4
....

5
....

Date:

1
....

2
....

3
....

4
....

5
....

Date:

1
....

2
....

3
....

4
....

5
....

Journalling

To connect with ourselves and define what's working and what isn't in our lives, it's so important to take a few moments every day to reflect.

The daily journal, with prompts, on the following pages is the perfect tool to help you connect with your feelings, practice gratitude, remind yourself of your goals, build confidence and keep a clear mind, day after day.

As I have shared already there is no right or wrong way to journal. Rather than using the following pages you may prefer to grab a beautiful notebook or some paper and just free write. You might choose to process your past or your present. Write out your affirmations, script your future dreams and desires. You might write your intentions for the day ahead or reflect on what went well and what you learnt as it draws to a close.

Here are a few journaling prompts that you could use if you would rather free write. These may reinforce the importance of implementing the strategies shared in each phase of the guide or help you identify some of your hidden stressors. They may inspire you to set some new goals or to create some more specific affirmations. Please don't feel you have to use these prompts.

> How do I want to feel at the end of this week? What are the steps I can create to make that happen?
> What would the best version of me do with her daily / weekly routines?
> What am I not doing daily that I could do to would enhance my health, happiness, success or wellbeing?
> Finish this sentence: "My life would be incomplete without …"
> What three things would you share with your teenage self?

Journalling

Date:

Today I'm feeling…	I'm grateful for…

The biggest challenges I have to deal with are…	I know I can overcome these because…

My goals for today are…

- ○ ....
- ○ ....
- ○ ....

- ○ ....
- ● ....
- ○ ....

Clear mind

Use this section to get everything that's on your mind onto paper so you can take the pressure off and feel more present, mindful and in charge.

....
....
....
....
....
....
....
....

Journalling

Date:

Today I'm feeling...	I'm grateful for...

The biggest challenges I have to deal with are...	I know I can overcome these because...

My goals for today are...

○ .... ○ ....

○ .... ● ....

○ .... ○ ....

Clear mind

Use this section to get everything that's on your mind onto paper so you can take the pressure off and feel more present, mindful and in charge.

....

....

....

....

....

....

....

....

Journalling

Date:

<table>
<tr><td>Today I'm feeling…</td><td>I'm grateful for…</td></tr>
<tr><td></td><td></td></tr>
</table>

<table>
<tr><td>The biggest challenges I have to deal with are…</td><td>I know I can overcome these because…</td></tr>
<tr><td></td><td></td></tr>
</table>

My goals for today are…

○ ....   ○ ....

○ ....   ● ....

● ....   ○ ....

Clear mind

Use this section to get everything that's on your mind onto paper so you can take the pressure off and feel more present, mindful and in charge.

....

....

....

....

....

....

....

....

Journalling

Date:

Today I'm feeling…	I'm grateful for…

The biggest challenges I have to deal with are…	I know I can overcome these because…

My goals for today are…

○ ....   ○ ....

○ ....   ● ....

● ....   ○ ....

Clear mind

Use this section to get everything that's on your mind onto paper so you can take the pressure off and feel more present, mindful and in charge.

....
....
....
....
....
....
....
....

111

Journalling

Date:

Today I'm feeling...	I'm grateful for...

The biggest challenges I have to deal with are...	I know I can overcome these because...

My goals for today are...

○ ....   ○ ....

○ ....   ● ....

○ ....   ○ ....

Clear mind

Use this section to get everything that's on your mind onto paper so you can take the pressure off and feel more present, mindful and in charge.

....

....

....

....

....

....

....

....

Journalling

Date:

Today I'm feeling…

I'm grateful for…

The biggest challenges I
have to deal with are…

I know I can overcome
these because…

My goals for today are…

○ ....

○ ....

○ ....

○ ....

○ ....

○ ....

Clear mind

Use this section to get everything that's on your mind onto paper so you can take
the pressure off and feel more present, mindful and in charge.

....

....

....

....

....

....

....

....

Journalling

Date:

<table>
<tr><td>

Today I'm feeling…

</td><td>

I'm grateful for…

</td></tr>
<tr><td>

The biggest challenges I
have to deal with are…

</td><td>

I know I can overcome
these because…

</td></tr>
</table>

My goals for today are…

○ ....   ○ ....
○ ....   ○ ....
○ ....

Clear mind

Use this section to get everything that's on your mind onto paper so you can take the pressure off and feel more present, mindful and in charge.

....

....

....

....

....

....

....

....

....

Lighten your load

We often weigh ourselves down with our thoughts and worrying about how we are going to resolve things or what to do next.

Use the space below to write down what you're 'carrying' in your mind, big or small. Take a good ten to fifteen minutes to do this exercise until you feel that you have unpacked the worries from your head. You may need to overspill if you are burdened with a lot. Once on paper it is often easier to realise your next best step or that things are not as big a worry as you thought when they were just in your head.

....

....

....

....

....

....

....

....

....

....

....

....

....

....

....

To-do or ta-da

Nothing feels as good as checking tasks off your to-do list and getting organised about what you need to work on every day. Use this space to turn that jumble of thoughts and to-dos in your brain into a clean and clear list. Give yourself clarity and peace of mind that everything is listed and taken care of.

If your 'to-do' list feels overwhelming or when you revisit it there is little to check off, use the 'ta-da' list to write down everything you have achieved today instead.

Please don't feel that you must fill the whole list in or tick everything off in one day. You might like to use a list for the week ahead and pick two to four tasks to complete each day.

Date:

To-do

Ta-da

To-do or ta-da

Date:

To-do	Ta-da

Date:

To-do	Ta-da

118

To-do or ta-da

Date:

| To-do | Ta-da |

Date:

| To-do | Ta-da |

To-do or ta-da

Date:

To-do	Ta-da

Date:

To-do	Ta-da

"Accept yourself, love yourself, and keep moving forward. If you want to fly, you have to give up what weighs you down."

Roy T. Bennett

The Women's Wellbeing Association is an online platform with **ONE** mission:

To support, encourage and motivate women in every area of their wellbeing; physically, mentally and emotionally

So many wonderful women feel exhausted and yet brush off their poor sleep, low mood, bloating and 'loss of self' feeling. They feel, amongst other things, overwhelmed, frustrated by their inch lost resistance, and lost - in both their confidence and self - above all they feel they are the only one feeling this way.

We create so much stress by our own emotions, usually the bottling up or playing down because we feel too alone to speak up. We believe it's just us feeling this way, that others have it all together, that it's only us experiencing the feeling of survival, low energy and troublesome hormonal symptoms. As a result, we put on a brave face while trying to spin all the plates when we're exhausted until we burn out or just snap.

Feeling energised and thriving (from surviving) is simply about taking the right next steps, learning the right holistic strategies and surrounding yourself with the right people.

Where could you be a year from today if you had access to the right information and SUPPORT? Find out more about the Womens Wellbeing Association at www.victoriajones.co.uk.

Thank you

My grandma always said, 'no one will ask how long it took', but I'll tell you anyway. This book has taken three years to get to print. I truly hope it doesn't take you as long to implement the suggestions in each phase as it took me to write them though.

As with all these things there have been people on the side lines, supporting and inspiring me and always believing in me. So, in true award ceremony style (without the trophy, stage and designer gown) I'd like to say thank you to some very special people.

Firstly my mum and dad. Thank you for always believing in me, supporting and guiding me. For doing all you have over the years to help me make my biggest dreams become reality.

Patrick, thank you for always reminding me who I am, what I am capable of and that "a winner never quits, and a quitter never wins".

Elaine, thank you for the hours of talking through ideas, okay the same idea another way. Thanks for inspiring me with your own women's wellness work and plans and for double checking my explanations when doubt crept in.

Spelling and punctuation have never been my speciality so huge thanks to Anne Skinner and Liz Guilford. Not only did these two amazing ladies keep me on track and believe in what I was creating, but they corrected spellings, changed punctuation and edited to make sure each phase and resource read right – sorry, read correctly.

Christa, thank you for contributing your gorgeous art to the reignite guide. You are such a talented and beautiful soul and I'm ecstatic you are here and so grateful our paths crossed and you trusted me with your own wellbeing.

Sue Stone – I did it! Thank you for constantly asking how the book was coming along and for believing in me, when I didn't believe in myself. Thank you for also teaching me to 'Love Life, Live Life'. The delay in writing this was potentially because of happy hour in Portugal, which I might not have entertained the idea of if it weren't for your teachings – okay well it was worth a try. The perfect time is now though.

And finally thank you to Jenny Burrell BSc (Hons), WHNC, SMRT. Founder and lead author / tutor of Burrell Education. The education that Jenny provides has been invaluable to me and without the 3rd Age and Menostrength programmes this would be a very short book. I am so grateful for the education and to be able to support women with their wellbeing because of it.

I am a firm believer that people come into your life for a reason, a season or lifetime. For those that who were, are and always will be part of my adventure, I thank you too.